Henry William Lucy

A Popular Handbook of Parliamentary Procedure

Henry William Lucy

A Popular Handbook of Parliamentary Procedure

ISBN/EAN: 9783744679466

Printed in Europe, USA, Canada, Australia, Japan

Cover: Foto ©Suzi / pixelio.de

More available books at **www.hansebooks.com**

A POPULAR HANDBOOK OF PARLIAMENTARY PROCEDURE

BY

HENRY W. LUCY

LONDON
GEORGE ROUTLEDGE AND SONS
BROADWAY, LUDGATE HILL
NEW YORK: 9 LAFAYETTE PLACE
1886

LONDON:
BRADBURY, AGNEW, & CO., PRINTERS, WHITEFRIARS.

TO

THE RIGHT HONOURABLE

SIR T. ERSKINE MAY, K.C.B.,

THE HIGHEST AUTHORITY ON PARLIAMENTARY PROCEDURE,

THIS LITTLE BOOK

Is Dedicated

WITH RESPECT AND ESTEEM.

PREFACE.

At the opening of the Parliament of 1880, an edition of this Handbook was published, but is now out of print. I have carefully revised it, bringing it down to the latest date, and have added two new chapters. The title sufficiently explains its object. It is an attempt to describe, in simple language and within moderate compass, the manner in which business is conducted in the House of Commons, and is especially designed to make the time-honoured intricacies of Parliamentary debate and procedure intelligible to the newspaper reader, who may not have access to the more elaborate and expensive authorities. It will also be found of some use to members of the Parliamentary Debating Societies which most big towns possess.

REFORM CLUB,
January, 1886.

CONTENTS.

CHAPTER I.

CHAPTER II.

CHAPTER III.

CHAPTER IV.

CHAPTER V.

CHAPTER VI.

CHAPTER VII.

CHAPTER VIII.

CHAPTER IX.

A

POPULAR HANDBOOK

OF

PARLIAMENTARY PROCEDURE.

CHAPTER I.

The Birth of Parliamentary Rules—The Sovereign and Parliament—Parliament and the Press—The Discipline of the House.

THE elaborate yet simple rules which guide Parliamentary procedure, which at one time seemed to fit all circumstances like a silken glove, and to control all episodes as with an iron vice, have had parallel growth with the establishment of the British Constitution. Parliament began to feel and exercise its great power in the reign of the Stuarts, and speedily found the necessity for making rules which should complete its influence by enabling it to control its own members. There are now among the Standing Orders of the House of Commons regulations made by the Parliament in which Cromwell sat, and others of the same date exist in a modified form. The fundamental principle of Parliamentary debate resolves everything within the narrow limits of a question put from the Chair, to be fully debated, sometimes amended, and, if necessary, divided upon. This procedure was settled in the reign of James I., and Shakespeare was alive when there was entered on the Journals of the House the standing order, "That nothing passes by order of the House without the question, and that no order be without the question affirmative and negative." This direction is observed to the present day in the minutest detail, and in the most formal manner.

A study of the forms of the House and of its manifold rules of debate would of itself constitute an interesting and instructive lesson in English history. It would be easy to trace the growth of the power of Parliament, synchronal with the establishment of the rights of the people, to observe its changing attitude towards the Crown, an attitude always effusively loyal—except where it has become necessary to go the other extreme, marked by cutting off a Sovereign's head. But, plainly discernible beneath this assumption of humility, has ever been the assertion of popular rights as opposed to monarchical aggression. There was a time, even so late as that of the Georges, when the sovereign had a very real and personal influence upon the action of Parliament. A Minister of State might be ordered to attend upon the Sovereign and directed straightway personally to convey to an opponent the seals and the insignia of office, of which he was himself relieved without notice, or without reason other than the King's whim. During the long series of years in which Mr. Gladstone and Mr. Disraeli were alternately in power, many circumstances have been taken into account in estimating from time to time how long one or the other was likely to retain office. But, between 1868 and 1874, for example, no one engaged in such speculation had occasion to consider the possibility of the Queen's sending for Mr. Gladstone, telling him she did not want him longer to be Prime Minister, and instructing him to go to Mr. Disraeli and inform him that he was thereafter to be Premier.

The times have changed marvellously, even within the last half century, and Parliament and its leaders are now answerable directly and solely to the people. In increasing measure the personal power of the Sovereign is becoming a myth. Nevertheless, the old forms remain intact; and when the newly elected Parliament shall be summoned, the Speaker standing humbly at the bar of the House of Lords will inform the representatives of the Sovereign that "in obedience to Her Majesty's commands, Her Majesty's faithful Commons in the exercise of their undoubted right and privilege have proceeded to the election of a Speaker, and as the object of their choice he now presents himself at your bar, and submits himself with all humility to Her Majesty's gracious approbation." The Speaker will be comforted with the assurance that "Her Majesty most fully approves and confirms him as the Speaker," which being happily arranged, the Speaker next by "humble petition to Her Majesty will pray that the Commons may be confirmed in all their undoubted rights and privileges."

This, now a mere form, was once a real thing, and in the very act of affirming the rights and privileges claimed with an almost servile submission to royal approval, we find that mixture of manly assertion and loyal obsequiousness before noted as full of significance to the student of English history. In earlier days the Speaker on these occasions, whilst soliciting approval of the choice of the Commons, was wont to add "that if it be Her Majesty's pleasure to disapprove of this choice, Her Majesty's faithful Commons will at once select some other member of their House better qualified to fill the station than himself." As the Commons grew in power this was more than they could stomach, and many years ago the phrase was quietly dropped.

It would be impossible to overstate the sacredness of the rules of the House of Commons as they are regarded by the House itself. The minutest and apparently the most trivial rule is sanctified by age, and if it has no particular bearing upon existing affairs, still it did its work in past ages, and possesses that claim upon attention and respect which a veteran of the Peninsular War holds upon the public of to-day. There is nothing the House shrinks from with more genuine horror than a proposal to alter an old rule of procedure. It will disestablish a church or pass a Reform Bill with a lighter heart than it will agree upon an amendment to a Standing Order affecting a particular procedure which Parliament has been in the habit of following since the Restoration. This is a wholesome feeling, and has its recommendation in the discipline and order which formerly existed within the House of Commons. But, at the same time, it is not without some inconvenience, and from time to time succeeds in placing an illustrious body in an undignified position.

Amongst the oldest and most deeply-rooted traditions of the House of Commons is the supposition that it carries on its debates in secrecy from the outer world. In this very year of grace and manifold newspapers, there is in existence in the House of Lords a standing order which declares: "That it is a breach of the privilege of this House for any person whatsoever to print or publish in print anything relating to the proceedings of the House without the leave of the House." This bears date February 27, 1698. On March 20, 1642, the House of Commons resolved: "That what person soever shall print or sell any Act or passages of this House, under the name of a diurnal or otherwise, without the particular license of this House, shall be reputed a high contemner and breaker of the privilege of Parliament, and shall be punished accordingly." In 1694 the Commons further ordered, "That no news-letter writers do, in their letters or other papers that they disperse, presume to intermeddle with the debates or any other proceedings of this House." Little more than a hundred years ago—on March 3, 1762—George III. having just ascended the throne, an order of equal stringency, one of a series promulgated during the previous century, was added to the Order Book of the House of Commons.

These orders remain unrepealed to this day; and as there exists nothing in the shape of an order recognising the service or the existence of the Press, it is presumable that the House would be able to act upon them, supposing an hon. member were to frame a suitable resolution. The relations of Parliament and the Press are in fact in an anomalous condition, which Englishmen would be the first to laugh at if they were brought under their notice as a story of a country beyond the sea. The bodily presence of representatives of the Press within the precincts of Parliament is recognised by both Houses in a manner which, though perhaps grudging, is nevertheless substantial—is satisfying if not satisfactory. There is a Press gallery in each House, with writing rooms and other conveniences for the use of reporters. Within the last dozen years the recognition of the Press by the House of Commons has taken the long stride indicated by the admission of the fact that representatives of the Press do not live upon pen-nibs or the bindings of their note-books; and eight or nine years ago an audacious First Commissioner of Works went the length of partitioning off a section of a corridor in which the representatives of the London journals might buy and eat cold meat at discretion. Early in the Parliament of 1880 reforms in the same direction, but on a much larger scale, were carried out. Upon the retirement of Colonel Forester, Assistant Serjeant-at-Arms, the lower portion of his residence was utilised as private rooms for Ministers whose convenience in this respect had been shamefully neglected. The upper part of the building was made over for the convenience of the Press, and a comfortable and well served dining-room provided together with additional writing-rooms. This circumstance, trivial in itself, may be the beginning of the end. But as yet the end is far off. The relations of the Press and Parliament are continually reaching a crisis, and of late scarcely a Session has passed over without a debate arising thereon. New members, struck with the grossness of the anomaly, attempt to reduce it to the basis of common sense; whereupon arises a debate which is instructive as showing how deeply rooted in the House of Commons is the antipathy towards changing a rule of procedure, even when no one finds it possible to defend it.

The rules relating to the Press are the only ones which challenge serious exception in the journals of the House of Commons. For the rest they are, in the main, devised with supreme wisdom, and formulated with singular skill, though it is true that in later years they have occasionally proved unequal to the strain of organised and unscrupulous obstruction. The best test of the successful adjustment of the machinery of debate in the House of Commons is for anyone intimate with its working to visit another assembly—any other in the world, from a vestry hall to Versailles, or from a meeting of a Town Council to a Session of the United States Congress. He cannot fail to be struck with the difference in the tone of the two assemblies, the advantage on the side of the House of Commons being due, first, to the existence of an admirable code of regulations; and secondly, to the obedience which even the most undisciplined member is fain to pay to their enforcement

What these rules are, and how they affect Parliamentary procedure, may perhaps be best illustrated by describing the House of Commons in detail. There are some men to whom procedure in the House of Commons is so familiar that it will seem puerile to enter upon a detailed explanation of words or phrases. But there are many more to whom, whilst the words and phrases are familiar enough, being daily met with in the course of newspaper reading, their meaning is absolutely unknown, or at best obscure. For the sake of completeness, and with due deference, I shall take the liberty of supposing that the reader knows absolutely nothing about procedure in the House of Commons.

CHAPTER II.

First Hours of a New Parliament—Summons to the Lords—Election of Speaker—Swearing-In—The Speech from the Throne—The Address.

ACTUALLY the first transaction that takes place at Westminster in connection with the assembling of a new Parliament is a meeting between the Clerk of the Crown in Chancery in Great Britain and the Clerk of the House of Commons. To the latter, the Clerk of the Crown solemnly hands a large roll,—that delivered in connection with the Parliament of 1886 will be the largest known in English history,—upon which is written the names of members returned to serve in Parliament. Members assemble at two o'clock, a motley crowd without a Speaker, a Chairman of Committees, or, in the event of a new Ministry having accepted office, a leader on the Treasury Bench. They are members of a House not yet constituted, and have no legislative functions. To the throng presently enters Black Rod with a message from the Lords Commissioners. In ordinary times the entrance of Black Rod is a solemn ceremony. At his approach the door is jealously closed, and it is only upon his peremptorily knocking and having satisfactorily answered the challenge that he is admitted. Then he marches up the floor of the House, thrice making lowly obeisance to the Mace, and with marked courtesy invites members of "this honourable House" to repair to the House of Lords. On the day of the meeting of a new Parliament, Black Rod assumes a jaunty, not to say a domineering manner. He bows to no one, has no reference to make to this honourable House, but simply invites or rather commands "gentlemen" to cross over to the other Chamber.

The procession of the Commons towards

the House of Lords is on this day different from ordinary occasions when the House is fully constituted. Then the Speaker in wig and gown, accompanied by his chaplain and preceded by the Serjeant-at-Arms with Mace on shoulder, goes with stately tread across the corridor, accompanied by a throng of members. As yet there is no Speaker, nor has the Mace emerged from the honourable obscurity in which it has remained since the dissolution. In answer to the summons from the Lords, the Clerk of the House goes first, and gentlemen struggle on behind, a tumultuous crowd, largely composed of new members who are determined not to miss anything.

Arrived in the House of Lords, the Commons, brought up at the Bar, behold seated on a bench under the shadow of the Throne five figures in red cloaks slashed with ermine, and having on their heads quaint three-cornered caps. Once more the Commons are reminded of their inchoate condition. Later in the session, when the Speaker and the Mace appear at the Bar in response to respectful summons, the five cloaked figures on the bench greet the visitors with stately courtesy, thrice uplifting their three-cornered hats. Now they slay the strangers with a stony stare, and curtly inform them that "it is her Majesty's pleasure that they shall forthwith proceed to the choice of some proper person to be their Speaker." Further, they are to present "such person" on the following day at two o'clock for her Majesty's royal approbation.

The crowd huddled in the narrow space below the Bar thereupon turn and race along the corridors, towards the House of Commons, anxious to obtain a seat for the approaching ceremony. When order is restored the Clerk at the Table rises and points with his finger towards some member with whom arrangement has been made to propose the election of a Speaker. On peril of his life, or at least his liberty, the Clerk must speak no word, but only dumbly point. The member thus indicated rises and proposes that such a member shall "take the chair of this House as Speaker." The motion is seconded, and is usually supported by the Leader of the House, and, if there is no contest, by the Leader of the Opposition. The formal question that the member thus designated do take the chair is not put, for the sufficient reason that there is no one to put it. The Speaker-elect is literally "called" to the chair. In response, he stands up in his place, and having expressed his sense of the honour proposed to be conferred upon him, submits himself to the House. He is again "called," and his proposer and seconder approaching him, conduct him to the chair.

This is presuming the most desirable case, rarely departed from in recent times, of the unanimous election of a Speaker. Should there be opposition, the two candidates, having been proposed and seconded, make a brief speech. Then the Clerk, now privileged to break the silence that has hung around him, puts the question that the member first proposed do take the Chair of this House as Speaker, and after this comes the division.

However elected, whether unanimously or after a division, the new Speaker is conducted to the Chair by his proposer and seconder. Standing on the upper step, he makes humble acknowledgment of the great honour conferred upon him, and beseeches the assistance of hon. members in carrying out the Rules of the House and preserving order. He seats himself in the Chair, and the Mace, which has hitherto lain *perdu*, is produced by the Serjeant-at-Arms and laid upon the table. Then follow congratulations, generally offered by the Leader of the House and the Leader of the Opposition, and the House straightway adjourns till the next day.

The stranger will not recognize from the

gallery the figure of the Speaker in long full-bottomed wig and flowing gown. The Speaker, like the butterfly, emerges by degrees from his chrysalis state. On the second day of a new Parliament he does not presume to reseat himself in the canopied chair which he had occupied for a few minutes on the previous day, nor does he array himself in full costume. He wears ordinary court dress, and what is known as a bob wig, in which costume he takes the chair at the table usually occupied by the Clerk of the House or the Chairman of Committees. Once more Black Rod appears, and with greater deference than was displayed on the day before, desires the immediate attendance of gentlemen in the House of Peers. The Speaker-Elect, followed by a mob of members, goes over to the House of Lords, and presenting himself at the Bar in the name and on behalf of the Commons of the United Kingdom, lays claim to their ancient and undoubted rights and privileges, especially to freedom from arrest and molestation for their persons and servants, to freedom of speech and debate, to free access to Her Majesty whenever occasion may require, and, finally and generally, that the most favourable construction may be put upon all their proceedings. The Lord Chancellor graciously assures him, in the name of the Queen, that this prayer shall be granted, and once more the Commons wend their way back to their own House.

It is one of the curious customs of Parliament that the Speaker always assumes that he has been in the House of Lords by himself, and that no one but he knows what took place there. Certainly he is always careful upon his return immediately to inform the Commons of the purport of his visit, telling them how he had been to the House of Lords where Her Majesty had been pleased, through her Commissioners, to approve the choice the House had made of him to be their Speaker, and how he had in their name and on their behalf, by humble petition to Her Majesty, laid claim to their ancient rights and privileges, which Her Majesty had confirmed to them in as full and ample manner as they have been heretofore granted or allowed by Her Majesty, or any of her Royal predecessors. Once more, for the third time, the Speaker makes respectful acknowledgment of the high honour the House had done him, and reminds members that the first thing is to take and subscribe the oath by law required. The Speaker sets the example, and standing upon the upper step of the chair solemnly takes and subscribes the oath. Next he signs the Roll of Parliament, and, retiring for a few moments, returns in the full dress of the Speaker.

Meanwhile two tables are brought in by the attendants, for the first and last time in the history of a Parliament permitted to cross the bar whilst the House is sitting. Copies of the oath and the Bible are sprinkled about the table. The first to take the oath and sign the Roll after the Speaker are the mover and seconder of the motion for his election. Then the Clerk at the Table proceeds to call upon members in alphabetical order of their constituencies, beginning with the counties, and in a few moments the tables are crowded. Six or eight members take hold of a copy of the Bible, and the Clerk of the House, standing at the head of the table reads the oath aloud, at the conclusion of which members kiss the book. They are then conducted by the Clerk to the Speaker, each one being introduced by name. The Speaker shakes hands with them, another batch come up to the table, and so hour after hour the proceedings monotonously meander to the end.

No record is kept of members who have been sworn in, and it will be seen that it would be quite easy for a member who for any reason did not want to take the oath, to evade the ceremony. If he took his seat on the next day, or the day following, it would be assumed that he had taken the oath, and there is certainly no one who has a right to question him. With members returned at bye elections the ceremony is more isolated, and, therefore, more notable, as was shewn in the various attempts made by Mr. Bradlaugh to take the oath. There is a resolution dated the 23rd of February, 1688, which to this day controls this matter. It directs that new members are to walk up the floor of the House between two members, making their obeisance as they go, "that they may be the better known to the House." Members seated upon a general election are not required to produce certificates that their return has been certified by the Clerk of the Crown to the Clerk of the House. That is done *en bloc*, and is taken for granted in individual cases. But every member returned to Parliament after a general election on coming to the table to be sworn must produce his certificate, a necessity which imposed a serious difficulty upon the present Lord Chancellor, Lord Halsbury, when, on the 6th of March, 1877, he, as Sir Hardinge Giffard, member for Launceston, came to be sworn in. The hon. and learned gentleman had left his certificate in his hat on the seat under the gallery where he had awaited the summons to the table, unmindful of which fact he proceeded in the presence of a crowded and hilarious House to search in his pockets for the missing document.

After the swearing-in of members has been completed, supposing the Government who had dissolved the late Parliament are confirmed in office, business proceeds in due course. But in the more common case of a change in the Government following upon the General Election, an adjournment takes place for a time sufficiently long to enable Ministers to secure their re-election. By a rule wholesome in its design but carried to a ludicrous length that demands early re-adjustment, members accepting direct from the Crown offices of profit thereby vacate their seats, and must seek re-election. When the new Ministers are thus confirmed in their places the House re-assembles and once more Black Rod, now with lowly obeisance and bated breath, appears upon the scene and "desires the presence of members of this honorable House to hear the Royal Speech read."

In the last hours of the Parliament of 1874 this procedure threatened a constitutional difficulty. Gen. Knollys was at that time Black Rod, and Sir George Bowyer, a great stickler for constitutional etiquette, had publicly taken note of the circumstance that Black Rod, contrary to established usage and the privilege of the Commons, had "required" the attendance of members at the House of Lords instead of "desiring" it. On the 24th of March, 1880, Black Rod came to deliver his last message to the Disraelian Parliament.

His mission was to bid their attendance in the other House, in order to hear the Lords Commissioners give their assent to certain Bills. What would he do on the present occasion? Would he deliberately affront the Commons, and if he did, would he be supported by the Lords, and would there be a conflict between two of the Estates of the Realm? Happily General Knollys did not prove contumacious, and the members present with a sigh of relief heard him "desire" their attendance, refraining from the more peremptory form which had aroused the indignation of Sir George Bowyer.

The Speaker, with the Mace borne before him, the Chaplain in his robe walking behind, the principal members of the Government following, and then a long array of members, proceed to the bar of the House of Lords, where the five cloaked figures on the bench before the Woolsack graciously acknowledge the Speaker's presence by saluting him three times. The Royal Commission having been read, the Lord Chancellor proceeds to read the Queen's Speech "in the Queen's own words" as he says, with a lack of veracity immemorial custom has consecrated. This done, the Speaker, the Mace, the Chaplain, Ministers and members return to their own House, where the Speaker, with that affectation of confidential communication already noted, informs the House where he has been, and having, as he says, "for greater accuracy," procured a copy of the Queen's Speech, he solemnly reads it word for word as if the members present had not been crowded at his back when five minutes earlier the Lord Chancellor read it in the Lords. But before the Speaker thus addresses the House a very curious and significant action is taken, so quietly that it probably escapes the notice of members. The Commons are well inclined to live on good terms with the other House, will even respond to their summons, and will be content with apparent humility to stand at their Bar. But the Commons of England are independent alike of the Crown and of the Peerage, and with intent to indicate this, some Bill is taken up and read a first time before the Commons will condescend to listen to report upon a matter comparatively so immaterial as the Speaker's visit to the House of Lords. When they have considered their own business, they will attend to the House of Lords and its proceedings.

As soon as the Speech has been read, a motion for an Address to Her Majesty is made and seconded. It is another of the quaint customs of the House of Commons that the proposer and seconder of the Address always appear in uniform. Gentlemen hitherto unsuspected of any connection with either of the services appear in military or naval uniform, and as some mild and blushing member rises in unaccustomed military array, the whispered enquiry goes along the benches,

"Who has tied Dolabella to this sword?" There are few tasks more difficult for a member of Parliament than that of moving the Address, unless it be the task of seconding it. There is no room for originality of speech or independence of thought. Like the Address itself, the speeches must be an echo of the document which the Lord Chancellor has read from the Woolsack "in the Queen's own words." It is practically the Ministerial programme of the legislative labours of the coming Session. The mover and seconder being Ministerialists *par excellence*, have only to echo the phrases of the Speech from the Throne.

But though there is a great deal of mummery and waste of time in the ceremony of moving and seconding the Address, the occasion itself is often one of serious import. This is the pretext upon which the Opposition, if they are so minded, give battle to Ministers. An amendment upon the Address is equivalent to a vote of censure on the Ministry, and if the amendment be carried, Ministers forthwith retire. In cases where such catastrophe is avoided, a select Committee is appointed to draw up the Address to be presented to Her Majesty in response to the Speech. The names of the Committee are recited by the Speaker, and the gentlemen called upon immediately leave the House, returning in suspiciously brief time with a lengthy Address which they report to the House, and it is forthwith accepted. The Address is an inane composition, which takes up, paragraph by paragraph, the Queen's Speech, echoing with approval its declaration. As a matter of fact, the men who prepare the Queen's Speech prepare the Address in reply, and it would be as unreasonable to expect the two documents to differ as it would have been to expect that the correspondence which Mr. Toots conducted with himself at Dr. Blimber's should be of a controversial character.

When the Queen has made a Speech from the Throne in person, the address is presented by the whole House, unless her Majesty should be in the country — where she generally manages to be on such occasions. The ceremony of presenting the Address by the whole House, now practically obsolete, was rather impressive. The Speaker, with a select number of members of the House, proceeded to the Palace, and being admitted to the Throne Room the Speaker read the Address to her Majesty, the members who moved and seconded it standing on his left hand. In the usual case of the Queen being in the country at the opening of Parliament the Address is formally lodged by certain members of the Privy Council.

When, in olden times, the Address had been presented by the whole House in the manner indicated, the Queen's answer was eported to the House by the Speaker. In recent times the formal reply to the Address is brought in by one of her Majesty's Household (usually the Comptroller), being a member of the House. He stands at the Bar, distinguished by his uniform, holding a white wand in his left hand and a roll in his right. The Speaker taking notice of him, he, standing at the Bar, reads the reply, all members uncovering. Having made an end of reading he advances up the floor of the House, bowing thrice, and hands the document to the Clerk at the table, who puts it in the bag whence it wends its way by due stages to the paper-mill. But long before the Queen's most gracious reply to the Address is returned, the Commons, emancipated from the trammels of the opening ceremony, have gladly got to work, and the clash of party warfare rings through the House.

CHAPTER III.

The Smallness of the House of Commons—The Best Time to see the House—Vested Interests—Private Business—First Readings—The House in Committee.

ONE of the first things that strikes a visitor to the House of Commons is, the smallness of the Chamber itself. The mind, accustomed to associate momentous events with Parliamentary debates, insensibly builds for honourable members a lordly pleasure-house. Perhaps no one who has read or thought much about the House of Commons has entered it for the first time without a feeling of disappointment. Much, of course, depends upon the time of the visit. When a great debate is on, when the floor of the House is densely crowded, and when honourable members, overflowing, fill the galleries that run the length of the Chamber there is no spectacle which, for intensity of interest and subdued excitement, can successfully compare with the House of Commons. But these occasions are rare, and the chances are much more in favour of a stranger entering the gallery at a moment when he may find the House represented by ten or fifteen gentlemen reclining in various attitudes of listlessness, whilst one addresses them at what promises to be interminable length.

The time when the House is certain to be seen in one of its best forms is at the hour of commencement of public business. Except on Wednesdays, when it meets at noon, or when special forenoon sittings are ordered on Tuesdays and Fridays, when it meets at two, or on occasional Saturdays at the end of the Session when there is no set hour for either beginning or ending—the House of Commons meets at a quarter to four.

The first business accomplished is the brief

religious service conducted by the chaplain. There is always a full muster at prayers, more especially when any interesting debate or episode is anticipated at a later period of the sitting. Doubtless a spirit of devotion is the principal incentive to this unanimity of action. But there is also a temporal advantage connected with the observance, and it may be here noticed, once for all, how, even in the smallest detail, the rules of the House are framed with the design to obtain a desirable end without the appearance of compulsion. The difficulty of seating in orderly fashion 670 gentlemen, who are in constant attendance throughout a Session of six months, appears a trivial matter, but is really full of subtle difficulties. As there are not 670 seats in the chamber, it obviously would be impossible definitely to assign a seat to each member, and even if it were possible, it would be unnecessary, as the attendance of members varies. It was essential to invent a self-adjusting rule, and this was done by the promulgation of the simple decree that members who desire to secure a seat for the evening may do so by being in attendance at prayer-time. To this end a small brass slide has been fixed in the back of each seat, and cards are provided on which a member may write his name, and so label a particular seat. This done, the seat is secured for the rest of the night, and he may claim it on returning from temporary absence of whatever duration.

Nearly every member of the House of Commons has his particular seat; but, with the exception of Ministers and ex-Ministers, he has no prescriptive right to it in continuity, and the inassailability of his tenure varies with his personal standing in the House. To mention two instances that will illustrate what is meant: Mr. Henley always sat on the corner seat of the third bench behind the Liberal Leaders. In the last Parliament Mr. Newdegate was, with equal regularity, to be found on the corner seat of the fourth bench below the gangway on the Opposition side. Neither of these gentlemen had any officially recognised right to his position, and Mr. Newdegate secured his only by unvarying punctuality at prayer-time. But no one would have thought of taking advantage of Mr. Henley's omission of the usual form to oust him from his place. Another bribe to devotion is that only those present at prayers are allowed to ballot for places in the Ladies' Gallery, for which there is great demand.

The House conducts its religious service with closed doors, but as soon as prayers are over, strangers are admitted. Private business is then proceeded with, and though it may extend over half-past four to whatever period of the evening may be necessary for its completion, public business may not, except by a resolution of the House, be commenced before half-past four. This rule, however, only holds good up to Easter, after which date private business is so much reduced that the hour is altered to a quarter past four.

"Private business" includes all Bills promoted by railway companies, gas companies, water companies, municipal corporations, or private individuals, and all measures of a purely local character. The metropolis is the only locality that is allowed to have its private Bills treated as public ones, which is, by the way, a great saving of expense to the metropolis. As far as Parliamentary procedure is concerned, transactions under this head are, with rare exceptions, purely formal in either House. Private Bills go through all the forms of public measures, with the exception that, whilst the latter are only occasionally referred to Select Committees, the former are invariably so dealt with. Public Bills, even if sent to a Select Committee, have still the ordeal of Committee of the whole House, whereas private Bills have not. In the House of Commons the first and second reading of a private Bill are, in almost all cases, matters of form and of course, though it is quite open to any member to oppose them at these stages. When a private Bill has been read a second time, it is relegated to a Select Cmmittee, where all the real business of consideration, amendment, acceptance, or rejection is accomplished. If a Select Committee pass a private Bill, it comes back to the House for a third reading, and is then sent on to the Lords or the Commons, according to the House in which it may have originated, and there goes through a similar course, previous to receiving the Royal assent. A public measure, whether brought in by a private member or by a Minister, can be introduced only after due notice has been given. A member announces that on a certain day he will move for leave to introduce a Bill. On the appointed day he makes the motion without—except in the case of important measures introduced from the Treasury Bench—making a speech.

Not in accordance with any written law, but as a matter of custom and courtesy, all Bills are allowed to pass their first reading unchallenged. Isolated cases occur when the rejection of a Bill is moved on its first reading. But a member taking such a course is expected to justify it by showing that there are exceptional and grave reasons for departing from the usage. Among the many suggestions made for easing the strain on the legislative machine, it has been proposed to modify this course, and to clear off in their initial stage measures which have no chance of becoming law. The advantage of this innovation would, however, chiefly affect the appearance of the order book. The time of the House occupied by the formality of asking and obtaining leave to introduce a Bill is infinitesimal. Leave obtained, the Bill is printed, and a day is named for the second reading, a stage at which the real tug of war commences.

When a Bill has passed its second reading, it is understood that the House approves its principle, and will consider its details. This is done in Committee of the whole House, an assembly which differs only in matters of form from the House of Commons itself. When *the House* is sitting, the Speaker presides, and the mace is laid upon the table. When the House goes into *Committee*, the Speaker retires, the mace is removed from the table, and the Chairman of Committees, a salaried officer elected with every Parliament, seats himself, not in *the* Chair, but at a chair at the head of the clerks' table.

The principal essential difference between procedure in Committee and in the House is that, whilst under the latter condition of affairs members may speak only once on a particular question, they may in Committee—and some do—address the Chair twenty or, if they please, a hundred times. One result of the reasonable application of this rule is, that the Committee is a more business-like body than the House itself. No man makes a speech to his constituents in Committee, or uses the Chairman as a telephonic means of communication with the listening world outside.

It often happens that not more than twenty or thirty men out of all the House of Commons remain at work upon a Bill in Committee. But these are the men out of the aggregate of 670 members who are practically acquainted with the subject matter. They talk in a conversational way, and argue points in a plain, earnest, business-like fashion, highly conducive to the accomplishment of good work. A Bill is talked over, clause by clause, and word by word, and when a Committee of the House of Commons has been quietly hammering away at it for several successive nights, the probabilities are that, in spite of party prejudices and personal interests—influences not absolutely unknown in application even to measures of public work-a-day interest—there has been fashioned about as good a piece of legislative workmanship as human skill, knowledge, and experience can devise.

CHAPTER IV.

Procedure in Committee—The Speaker and the Chairman—Naming Members—Notices of Motion—Balloting for Precedence—An Ingenious Conspiracy.

A BILL cannot be rejected in Committee, though it may be so emasculated by the rejection or alteration of an important clause that its promoters may deem it useless to proceed further with it. Failing this extreme course, the Committee, having gone through a Bill, clause by clause, and amended it or approved it, the Chairman "reports it to the House." At this stage fresh debate may arise, new clauses may be added, clauses approved in Committee may be rejected, or the Bill may be thrown out. If it escape this ordeal, it is ordered to be read a third time, when its opponents, if they can even now muster a majority, may yet throw it out. Having passed a third reading, it is sent up to the House of Lords, where it goes through all these processes over again. If the Lords make any alteration, the Bill will return to the House of Commons, who will consider the Lords' amendments. There remains only the Royal assent, which given, the Bill becomes an Act, and is added to the statute book.

It may be mentioned here that, while under all circumstances the Speaker is invariably addressed and alluded to by his title, the Chairman of Committees is, when actually in the Chair, always addressed by name. Addressing members by name or alluding to them by name is a breach of order more quickly resented than any other. Yet, there are times when names may be used without exciting a burst of indignation. Thus, when a member nominates a Select Committee, he mentions the proposed members by name. But he may do so only when, at the outset, he recites the names in catalogue. If he, or any other member, alludes to the nominees in the course of his speech, he must designate them by the name of the constituencies they represent. In the same way, when the Speaker calls upon a member to address the House, he names him. But should the Speaker refer to a member in the course of any observations he may offer on points of order—the only topics open to him—he must use the Parliamentary mode of reference.

This seems a small matter, but it is not without its significance and practical use. It helps in no slight degree to maintain throughout the speeches a tone of high courtesy, or, at worst, of animosity decently disguised. An hon. member, if he were at liberty to talk about Mr. Biggar, for example, might, out of the fulness of his heart, lapse into expressions which would considerably lower the standard of debate. But by the time he has given utterance to the resonant phrase "the hon.

member for Cavan," he has time to recollect the circumstances under which he speaks, and so modifies his expressions. Out of the House, members are of course at liberty to refer to each other by name, and any newspaper taken up during the flow of recess oratory will show how different is the tone of personal reference as compared with that dignified style which prevails where "all are honourable" members.

Through the first half of the session the amount of private business is sufficient fully to occupy the preliminary half-hour. But, as already stated, soon after the Easter Recess, the amount of private business has usually been so far diminished that a quarter of an hour is, on the average, found sufficient for its disposal, and a resolution is proposed and agreed to that public business shall commence at a quarter past four.

The business of the House of Commons for each evening is set forth in an agenda called

"The Orders of the Day." The first procedure, after the Speaker's cry of "Order! order!" follows upon the stroke of half-past four and announces the commencement of public business, is the giving of notices of motion. It is, of course, desirable that a favourable occasion should be seized by a member having charge of a motion, and there is consequently much manœuvring for precedence. The stranger in the gallery will hear the Speaker call out the name of members in what appears to be chance succession. The member addressed will thereupon arise, read out his notice, and give place to another in quite a different part of the House, upon whom the eye of the Speaker may, still by chance as it appears, next have fallen. But no place is left for chance in English Parliamentary procedure.

What really happens in respect of notices of motion is this;—On the table at which the clerks sit there lies a long sheet of paper, ruled, and having printed figures down the side of it. Members desiring to give notice of motion go up to the table, and write their names on this list. Small bits of paper, bearing numbers corresponding to those on the list, are twisted up and placed in a box before the clerk. When "notices of motion" are called on, the clerk puts his hand in the box, and draws out one of the pieces of paper, calling aloud the number he finds thereon—say the figure is 44, and that, to use a name not unfamiliar on the notice paper, Mr. Parnell has chanced to write his name on the line numbered 44. The clerk calls out the number; the Speaker, who has meanwhile been furnished with the list of names, on referring to it, finds that Mr. Parnell is number 44, and thereupon calls him by name. Mr. Parnell thus has the first choice of unoccupied days within the period of one month from the date of the sitting. The process is repeated till the contents of the box are exhausted, and the list of notices of motion is concluded. Motions are taken in the House in the order in which notice has been given, and it is obviously a matter of prime importance to obtain a good position.

Before placing his name on the notice-paper, and awaiting the chance of the ballot, a member will have carefully studied the order book, and will have ascertained what days within the month have already been appropriated. It will, in fact, be necessary to have obtained a perfect mastery of the chronology of desirable days, for it is only in case he has the good fortune to be called first, that he has a tolerable choice, or on Tuesdays and Fridays a full choice. If he is second or third on the ballot list, hon. members who have gone before will naturally have taken the best days, and he must, without a moment's hesitation, make his selection from the remainder. It often happens that, when there is a long list of notices of motion, members who have placed their names on the list, and who are not called till after ten or a dozen members have made their selection, postpone their intention of fixing a day. Whereupon will be seen the phenomenon, so perplexing in the Strangers' Gallery, of hon. members called upon by name and answering only by taking off their hats and saluting the Speaker.

In the session of 1876 an ingenious conspiracy was entered upon by the Home Rule members, with the object of obtaining what the Speaker subsequently stigmatised as 'an unfair advantage' in respect of precedence for notices of motion. They had agreed upon a group of some ten subjects which they desired to bring under the notice of the House. There being at the time about forty Home Rulers in attendance at the House, copies of these ten motions were placed in the hands of each, with a common understanding as to which it was most desirable to give preference,

The whole forty then wrote their names down on the notice-paper, and of course each had a chance in the ballot box. On the names being called out, the first Home Ruler who got a place gave notice to move for leave to introduce the particular measure, or to move the particular resolution, which it had been privately agreed was of prime importance. The second man called secured the next best place open for the measure of second importance, and so on, through the list. The chances of any particular measure which the Home Rulers had in charge were thus exactly forty to one against the opportunity of any measure which any other private member advocated. The plan succeeded admirably, and the House was mystified and surprised at the good luck which attended Home Rule members, and secured for them the best nights of the session. Some weeks later, when all the mischief was done, Captain Ritchie drew the attention of the Speaker to the facts. But the Home

Rulers were able to bear with equanimity the solemn rebuke of the right hon. gentleman, for they had gained all they wanted, at least for the session.

CHAPTER V.

Private Days and Public Days—"On Going into Committee of Supply"—Forcing a Division—The Previous Question.

ABSOLUTELY the most favourable position for a private member having charge of a resolution is the first place on the orders for a Tuesday night, though the satisfaction of a successful balloter who has secured this place is tempered by the possibility of being counted out. The best chance for a private Bill is first place on Wednesday. The days open to private members having charge of motions are Tuesdays, Wednesdays, and Fridays, Wednesdays being confined to Bills. Mondays and Thursdays are Government nights. Wednesday is a bad day for a member who desires to bring a Bill to an issue, unless he has first place, because, as all discussion peremptorily closes at a quarter to six, if he begins late his opponent may shelve him by the simple expedient of continuing to talk till the hand of the clock touches the quarter, when, as if he were part of the clock machinery, the Speaker will rise and declare the debate adjourned. By determined talking this may happen even to the Bill that is first on the list. In some respects, Friday is a better night than Tuesday, the average of counts out being considerably less. Committee of Supply is always the first order of Friday night, and private members bring on their grievances in the form of amendments to the main proposition. Thus, if the Government want money, it is their interest to keep a House in the expectation that, when all the notices of motion are disposed of, what they regard as the real business of the evening will commence.

These remarks apply to the member who has obtained the first place on the Orders. For the second, and still more for others who may follow, there is a danger peculiar to Friday nights, which makes the date one to be avoided. Friday is nominally a Government night, and, as I have said, the first order of the day is always Supply; that is to say, Government desire to move the House into Committee, in order to obtain votes of money on account of the various Services. But, in accordance with the constitutional maxim which concedes to Englishmen an opportunity of grumbling when they are about to pay money, it is a rule of the House that private members may bring forward what they hold to be grievances in the shape of amendments to the main proposition, which is, that the House shall go into Committee of Supply. The member who has obtained the first place on the list brings forward his grievance, has it debated, and probably divides the House upon it. It is the custom of the House of Commons to divide always on the original question, and the proposition put from the chair on Friday nights is 'that I do now leave the chair.' If that is negatived, the next thing done is to put the amendment as a substantive motion, and, except in cases of wilful obstruction, the House does not divide again, but accepts the amendment. In these circumstances the position of the member who stands second on the list is vastly improved. The motion to go into Committee is made again, and he brings forward his particular grievance, which he has formulated in the shape of an amendment, and which may be pressed to a division.

But supposing, as generally happens, the Government, opposing the first amendment, defeat it in the division lobby, or cause it to be negatived without division. In either case none of the succeeding amendments on the paper can be urged to a division. The question before the House is, that it shall resolve itself into Committee of Supply. That has been agreed to upon a division, or by negativing the amendment, and there is an end to the matter. But whilst they may not take the opinion of the House on the questions they bring forward, members who follow with amendments may have them fully debated, and, as many a dreary and profitless Friday night testifies, they are not slow to avail themselves of this privilege. Of late an attempt has been made to qualify the state of affairs by establishing the rule that the subject-matter of motions brought forward on going into Committee of Supply must relate to the particular Service on account of which money is to be voted. This, however, is limited to Mondays, and has merely the effect of classifying the debates, and has in no degree stopped the aggregate torrent of talk.

This rule with respect to Friday nights opens a field for a good deal of party manœuvring, in which the Government of the day have the whip hand. An amendment standing second or third on the list may be one on which it would be exceedingly awkward to divide. The first amendment offers a convenient and infallible means of avoiding the dilemma. The mover may have been 'got at' by those who would force the obnoxious division, and he may, at the conclusion of the debate, express himself satisfied, and refuse to divide. If he were allowed to withdraw his amendment the critical motion No. 2 would follow, and the pending division would take place upon it. But there are ways of forcing a division; and a single member refusing his assent to the withdrawal of an amendment duly moved can, even against the expressed wish of the rest of the House, have the question put from the Chair. If he can find a co-teller, he can even force a division. Failing that, the purpose hinted at is nevertheless accomplished, for when the question has been put and the House has, by its unchallenged voice, declared its desire to go into Committee, the issue is as completely settled as if a division had taken place, and consequently none of the subsequent amendments can be put to the vote.

Sometimes a motion is opposed by moving 'the previous question.' This is usually done when the objection is rather addressed to the opportuneness of the time of moving than to the substance of the motion; and the mode of putting the question to the House is very puzzling, even to members of considerable experience.

CHAPTER VI.

Putting the Question—Preparing for a Division—A Minority of One—The Tellers—The Sand-glass—Who cut the Bell-wire?—"Ayes to the Right, Noes to the Left"—The Division Lobbies—Announcing the Figures—The Casting Vote.

A QUESTION in the House of Commons is decided either by voice or vote. When a debate is brought to a conclusion, the Speaker rises and reads aloud the motion which has been brought forward. If there is an amendment, he reads that also; but what the House first divides on is always the original question. Say, to take the briefest form of question, that the original motion was the second reading of the Church Steeple Bill. The Speaker will say, "Church Steeple Bill; the original motion was that the Bill be now read a second time, since which an amendment has been made to leave out the word 'now,' and insert 'on this day six months.' The question is, that this Bill be now read a second time." On this formula the House divides. If the majority be in the affirmative, the Bill is ordered to be read a second time. If the majority be the other way, the main proposition is declared lost, and the Speaker, immediately upon reading the figures of the division, says, "The question is, that this Bill be read a second time this day six months." Under ordinary circumstances, the Opposition accept their defeat, and do not raise their voice against the decision of the Speaker, that "the ayes have it." But they may, if they please, divide again on this question, and may even raise a fresh debate upon it. If no amendment has been moved, the question is put "that the Bill be now read a second time."

When the Speaker has put a proposition before the House, he invites those in favour of it to say "aye," and those who oppose it to say "no." Then follow two responsive shouts, and forming a judgment on the respective volumes of sound, the right hon. gentleman declares that he thinks "the ayes have it," or "the noes have it," as the case may be. Should this decision be challenged, even by a single voice, the House will be cleared for a division. If the dissentient voice is literally one, the Speaker will ask the hon. member to name a teller. If he cannot do so, the ruling of the Speaker becomes final, as on a division there must be two tellers on each side. But the House *must* divide if there are two tellers, even though, as happened more than once during the campaign of obstruction in the last Parliament, there be none for them to tell.

During the debate on Dr. Kenealy's motion for re-opening the case of the Claimant, Major O'Gorman saved Dr. Kenealy, and his co-teller, Mr. Whalley, from the queer eminence of having constituted themselves tellers in a division wherein—worse plight than that of the needy knife-grinder—they had no followers to tell. Amid uproarious cheers, the Major emerged from the otherwise empty lobby devoted to the "ayes," representing in his person the full numerical strength of the minority.

On party divisions, the tellers are the Whips on either side. In divisions on questions raised by private members and opposed by the Government, the mover and seconder tell for "the motion," and the Ministerial Whips for "the Government." A division being insisted on, the Speaker directs strangers to withdraw, and simultaneously a sand-glass, which stands on the clerks' table, is turned, and through all the passages and Committee Rooms of the House is heard the tinkling of the electric bell. Formerly the order for strangers to withdraw was literally carried out, the strangers' galleries being cleared. But now only the seats under the gallery, to which a few strangers are admitted by special order, are cleared—a reasonable precaution, seeing that these seats are actually on the floor of the House, and (as has happened, at least once, according to well-authenticated history) a stranger straying into the lobbies might actually figure as a unit in the division list. The sand-glass takes two minutes to run out, during which time the bells are furiously twanging all over the House, and hon. members, who have been in the reading room, library, dining room, or even out on the terrace, come hurrying in to vote.

When St. Stephen's Club was opened, its proximity to the House suggested the convenience of connecting it with the system of division bells, so that supporters of the Government, accustomed to congregate there, might have due notice of a pending division. One night, during the session of 1875, a Bill, in which the Home Rule members were deeply interested, was in Committee. The supporters of the Government were so far amenable to the injunctions of the Whip that they would come in to vote; but they positively declined to remain to hear the debate. Thus, whenever a clause was reached on which a division was challenged, there was the sound of hurrying feet along the subway that connects the Club with the House, and an overwhelming contingent of hon. members arrived to vote down the opposition. About eleven o'clock a most important clause was reached, and a division was challenged. The electric bells rang out the usual summons; but, to the consternation of Sir William Dyke and Mr. Winn, and to the unutterable indignation of Sir Michael Hicks-Beach, then Secretary for Ireland, the Ministerial majority mysteriously diminished, and even vanished, the Home Rulers carrying their point. Upon investigation, it was discovered that something had happened to the communication between the division bell of the House and the bell in

St. Stephen's Club—it was in the days of the late Mr. Ronayne, who was a practical engineer as well as a man of great humour—and the indignation of the Ministerial Whip was equalled only by the consternation of the contingent of hon. members at the Club when they heard there had been a division.

When the last grain of sand in the glass has run out, the Speaker rises and cries, "Order! order!" This is a signal to the doorkeepers to close and lock the doors, and members arriving thereafter cannot vote. This, it may be mentioned, touches the precise meaning of the small paragraph frequently seen in the newspapers on the morning after a division in respect of which constituencies are likely to look up the division list to see how their member voted. When Mr. Marmaduke Montblanc is "accidentally shut out from the division lobby, and prevented from voting" in such and such a division, it simply means that Mr. Marmaduke Montblanc was dining, or smoking a cigar on the terrace, or was writing letters whilst the debate was going on, and was not able to arrive at the House before the door was shut.

The doors being locked and profound silence reigning within the House, the Speaker proceeds to put the question as above described. He again takes the sense of the House by the cry of "aye," and "no," and declares which way according to his opinion, the majority goes. It sometimes happens that the spirit of sportiveness which is always latent in the House of Commons has suggested the pushing of matters to this extreme, and that there is no real intention of going to a division. In these circumstances the Speaker's ruling is not challenged a second time, and the motion is declared to be either negatived or carried without a division. Should the division be persisted in, the Speaker directs "the ayes to the right," "the noes to the left," and names the tellers for either party.

Outside the Chamber, and running parallel with its length, are the division lobbies. Into one or other of these, according as they vote "aye" or "no," the members pour. The tellers make their way in pairs to the head of the lobbies, a teller for the ayes pairing off with a teller for the noes, an arrangement which prevents contention as to results. Members pouring in at one end of the lobby work their way up to the other, at which stands a wicket guarded by two clerks, who have on a desk large pieces of pasteboard, on which are the names in alphabetical order of every member of the House. It is the business of these clerks to know every member by sight; and, as each passes through the wicket, his name is ticked off on the list.

A few paces further on, the two tellers stand face to face; and, as the members pass between them, one of the tellers calls aloud the growing numbers. When the last member has passed through, the ticked pasteboard is sent off to the printers to appear next morning as the division list, and the tellers entering the House communicate in turn the figures to the clerk at the table, who writes them down on a piece of paper, which he hands to the principal teller for the majority. The four tellers walking some paces down the floor of the House turn round, and advancing abreast towards the Speaker, with obeisance twice repeated, the teller who holds the paper reads out the figures. The paper is then handed to the Speaker, who also reads out the result of the division, adding, "the ayes have it," or "the noes have it," according as the majority have gone.

Neither the Speaker nor the Chairman of Committees, being actually in the chair, votes unless the division result in a tie, when the President gives the casting vote. This is a contingency which does not frequently arise, but it has happened more than once under circumstances of great excitement. To cite two instances of comparatively recent date—the Church Rates Abolition Bill was, in the Session of 1861, thrown out by the casting vote of the Speaker, and in 1864, the Tests Abolition (Oxford) Bill was read a third time through the intervention of the same agency.

CHAPTER VII.

Talking out a Bill — Morning Sittings — Counting Out — "Forty!"—Counts-out in Committee.

A BILL or a Resolution may be got rid of with equal effect by other means than a vote. Wednesday afternoon, as has already been hinted, offers facilities for shelving a measure, which, if used to the full, cannot fail of success, as was shown on a memorable occasion in the Session of 1877, when the House, meeting at four o'clock on a Tuesday afternoon, sat till after six on the following day, having remained in session for twenty-six and a half hours. There is no recognised limit as to the duration of a sitting on Monday, Tuesday, Thursday, or Friday.

In the case of a morning sitting, the House

meets at two o'clock and the sitting is suspended at seven, being resumed at nine, when it may proceed indefinitely. But on Wednesday the House meets at twelve, and must, unless the Standing Order be suspended by special vote, adjourn at six. The measure of discussion is limited by the reduction of a quarter of an hour, and at a quarter to six—even though a member addressing the House be in the middle of a sentence—the Speaker rises and calls on the next business, the debate thus interrupted being adjourned. As a matter of form, the adjournment takes place till the "next day." As a matter of fact, it is indefinite; for, every available day of the Session being appropriated, the member in charge of the Bill has no chance of renewing the discussion.

Thus, if a Bill be brought in on a Wednesday, an adversary may, single-tongued, succeed in throwing it out, even though the House should otherwise unanimously desire to pass it. There is a well-authenticated case of a member (the late Mr. Vincent Scully), who rose to move the rejection of a Bill at one o'clock on Wednesday afternoon. Whilst keeping strictly within the forms of the House, he indulged in a long dissertation which lasted up to a few seconds of a quarter to six. Turning towards the clock and noting the precise moment, the hon. member observed: "After these few preliminary observations I will now proceed to consider the principle of the Bill." Whilst he was yet uttering the sentence, the hand of the clock touched a quarter to six, the Speaker rose, and the debate was adjourned.

Another weapon in the armoury of Opposition is the "count out," perhaps one of the most useful agencies in Parliamentary procedure. A quorum in the House of Commons consists of forty members; and, of course, no business may be discussed save in the presence of a quorum. But, as a matter of fact, a great deal of business is accomplished, or, at least, a great many hours are got through by the House of Commons, in the presence of from five to fifteen gentlemen. The non-existence of a quorum is a circumstance of which the Speaker does not take notice unless his attention be directly called to it. It was formerly the practice of a member desiring to bring about "a count" to approach the Speaker covertly from behind his chair, and whisper in his ear, and it was the etiquette of Parliamentary reporters not to mention the name of the often welcome interloper. Of late years the more manly practice is growing for members to rise in their place, and openly call the Speaker's attention to the fact that there are not forty members present.

However the process be accomplished, the Speaker immediately rises, and announces that his "attention has been called to the members present," concluding with the injunction that "strangers will withdraw."

Thereupon takes place the procedure described in connection with a division. The sand-glass is turned; the electric bells rattle throughout the House the announcement of the imminence of a count; and the same interval of two minutes is allowed to members to congregate. A count, however, differs from a division, inasmuch as the doors are left open, and members coming in whilst the Speaker is counting are included in the members, and sometimes save the House. When the sand is run out, the Speaker begins to count, using his cocked hat to point to individual members as he enumerates. He counts audibly, pointing to each member in succession. If he finds forty members on the benches, he, without remark, resumes his seat, and the interrupted orator proceeds. If there are less than forty, he concludes the enumeration with the cabalistic words, "the House will now adjourn;" and, forthwith, at whatever hour it be, the House adjourns, and the motion and its advocate are effectually disposed of.

It sometimes happens that the House may be adjourned upon a count, through the process of a division. If the House divides, and the division list shows an aggregate of voters less than forty, the absence of a quorum is demonstrated, and the House forthwith adjourns. Counts can also take place in Committee. But if it be found that forty members are not present, an adjournment does not thereupon take place. The Speaker is sent for, the fact is reported to him, and he again counts. Sufficient members to form a quorum may, by this time, have arrived, in which case the Committee resumes. But if it should still be found that there are not forty present, an adjournment takes place.

CHAPTER VIII.

Necessity for doing Something—Increase of Business—Epidemic of Speech-making—Special Wires—A Reported Speech that was Never Delivered—Asking Questions.

THESE rules of debate and these formulæ of procedure have enabled Parliament to carry on the business of the nation through two centuries. There have been occasional hitches, which had led to proposals of reform. Sometimes a little tinkering has been permitted, and in 1882 a winter Session was devoted to the work with what result the next chapter shows. But oftener Lord Melbourne's historical suggestion, "Can't you let it alone?" has been followed. The time is, however, not far distant, when the urgent necessity for again considering the forms of Parliamentary procedure with the view of establishing permanent reform will be frankly acknowledged and boldly met.

The rules of debate were made at a time when the business of the Legislature was infinitely less extensive and less complicated than at present. Business has increased with the growth of the nation; and, even in enlarged degree, has grown the capacity for talk. There was a time when speech-making in the House of Commons rested with a few tongues. Infinitely the larger proportion of members were content to put in an appearance during a debate, and to vote when required. But the extension of the press, and, above all, the institution of Special Wires as a medium of communication between the metropolis and provincial newspapers, have changed all that.

We are naturally loth to acknowledge the potency of small matters in great connections. It is nevertheless a fact that the creation of the Special Wire is an event which has had a serious effect upon Parliamentary procedure. Men will not often speak in an assembly which will not hear them, nor before representatives of the Press who do not notice them. But the cheapening of telegraphic communication, leading to the institution of Special Wires, has created a system by which speeches of members are reported verbatim in the local newspapers. Thus we have members speaking, not to the House of Commons, but to their constituencies; a state of affairs which, whilst it adds to the inherent dreariness of a particular speech, makes its delivery imperative. In former days, when a man had prepared a speech, and found that the House was determined not to hear it, he, after a fair show of resistance, was accustomed to give way. Now, when a member has prepared a speech, he takes into consideration the circumstance that the papers which his constituents read have made arrangements for fully reporting it. The local journal may, indeed, as has happened in recent Parliamentary history, already have the speech in type; whence it becomes clear that the speech must be recited, though the Heavens fall, amid the clamour of an angry House.

Another tendency which serves to lengthen proceedings in Parliament, and to shorten the time for doing business, is the habit of asking questions, not necessarily trivial in themselves, but, when put in the Imperial Parliament, suggestive of wasted human breath and intellect. This has grown enormously within the last twenty years, as statistics will show. In 1857, 451 questions were put during the Session. In 1867, they were more than doubled, amounting to 912. In 1877 they were trebled, reaching the number of 1,343. A corresponding increase in the actual time of the sitting has followed upon this development of Parliamentary curiosity. In 1857 the House sat 903 hours. In 1867, it sat 1,043 hours; and in 1877, it sat 1,200 hours, less one. What this process of asking questions means will appear on consideration of the fact that, in 1877, upwards of 80 hours, a period of time equal to two full Parliamentary weeks, were occupied in asking questions and answering them! In later sessions, up to and specially inclusive of 1885, this proportion has vastly increased. When we take into consideration that the putting of questions is often the preliminary step to raising a discussion, it will appear that herein lies a useful clue to the much-deplored loss of time in Parliament.

CHAPTER IX.

An Autumn Session—The New Rules—How they have Worked —How affected by Changes in New Parliament.

In the winter of 1882, the House of Commons, goaded to desperation by the successful tactics of the obstructionists, met in special session, determined to deal once for all with the condition of disorder into which the assembly had been brought by the action of a small body of men who cared neither for the Speaker nor for public opinion. The result of protracted labours is embodied in the following new rules, which are now incorporated with the Orders of Procedure in the House of Commons.

1. *Putting the Question.*—When it shall

appear to Mr. Speaker, or to the Chairman of Ways and Means in a Committee of the whole House, during any debate, that the subject has been adequately discussed, and that it is the evident sense of the House, or of the Committee, that the question be now put, he may so inform the House or the Committee; and, if a motion be made "That the question be now put," Mr. Speaker, or the Chairman, shall forthwith put such question; and, if the same be decided in the affirmative, the question under discussion shall be put forthwith: Provided that the question, "That the question be now put," shall not be decided in the affirmative, if a division be taken, unless it shall appear to have been supported by more than two hundred members, or unless it shall appear to have been opposed by less than forty members and supported by more than one hundred members.

2. *Motions for Adjournment before Public*

Business.—No motion for the adjournment of the House shall be made until all the questions on the Notice Paper have been disposed of, and no such motion shall be made before the Orders of the Day, or Notices of Motions have been entered upon, except by leave of the House, unless a member rising in his place shall propose to move the adjournment, for the purpose of discussing a definite matter of urgent public importance, and not less than forty members shall thereupon rise in their places to support the motion; or unless, if fewer than forty members and not less than ten shall thereupon rise in their places, the House shall, on a division, upon question put forthwith, determine whether such motion shall be made.

3. *Debates on Motions for Adjournment.*—When a motion is made for the adjournment of a debate, or of the House, during any

debate, or that the Chairman of a Committee do report progress, or do leave the Chair, the debate thereupon shall be confined to the matter of such motion; and no member, having moved or seconded any such motion, shall be entitled to move, or second, any similar motion during the same debate.

4. *Divisions.*—After the House has entered upon the Orders of the Day or Notices of Motions, when, after the House has been cleared for a division, upon a motion for the adjournment of a debate, or of the House during any debate, or that the Chairman of a Committee do report progress, or do leave the Chair, the decision cf Mr. Speaker, or of the Chairman of a Committee, that the Ayes or Noes have it is challenged, Mr. Speaker or the Chairman may, after the lapse of two minutes, as indicated by the sand glass, call upon the members challenging to rise in

their places, and, if they be less than twenty in a House of forty members or upwards, he may forthwith declare the determination of the House or of the Committee.

5. *Irrelevance or repetition.*—Mr. Speaker, or the Chairman of Ways and Means, may call the attention of the House, or of the Committee, to continued irrelevance or tedious repetition on the part of a member; and may direct the member to discontinue his speech.

6. *Postponement of Preamble.*—In Committee on a Bill, the Preamble do stand postponed until after the consideration of the Clauses, without question put.

7. *Chairman to leave the Chair without Question.*—When the Chairman of a Committee has been ordered to make a report to the

House, he shall leave the Chair without question put.

8. *Half-past Twelve o'Clock Rule.*—That, except for a Money Bill, no Order of the Day or Notice of Motion be taken after half-past Twelve of the clock at night, with respect to which Order or Notice of Motion a Notice of Opposition or Amendment shall have been printed on the Notice Paper, or if such Notice of Motion shall only have been given the next previous day of sitting, and objection shall be taken when such Notice is called. That motions for the appointment or nomination of Standing Committees and Proceedings made in accordance with the provisions of any Act of Parliament or Standing Order, motions for leave to bring in Bills, and Bills which have passed through Committee of the whole House, be excepted from the operation of this Order. Provided, That

every such Notice of Opposition or Amendment be signed in the House by a member, and dated, and shall lapse at the end of the week following that in which it was given. Provided also, That this Rule shall not apply to the nomination of Select Committees.

9. *Order in Debate.*—Whenever any member shall have been named by the Speaker, or by the Chairman of a Committee of the whole House, immediately after the commission of the offence of disregarding the authority of the Chair, or of abusing the Rules of the House by persistently and wilfully obstructing the business of the House, or otherwise, then, if the offence has been committed by such member in the House, the Speaker shall forthwith put the question, on a motion being made, no amendment, adjournment, or debate, being allowed, "That such Member be suspended from the service of the House;"

and if the offence has been committed in a Committee of the whole House, the Chairman shall, on a Motion being made, put the same question in a similar way, and if the Motion is carried shall forthwith suspend the proceedings of the Committee and report the circumstance to the House; and the Speaker shall thereupon put the same question, without amendment, adjournment, or debate, as if the offence had been committed in the House itself. If any member be suspended under this Order, his suspension on the first occasion shall continue for one week, on the second occasion for a fortnight, and on the third, or any subsequent occasion, for a month: Provided always, That suspension from the service of the House shall not exempt the member so suspended from serving on any Committee for the consideration of a Private Bill to which he may have been appointed before his suspension: Provided also, That not more than one member shall be named at the same time, unless several members, present together, have jointly disregarded the authority of the Chair: Provided always, That nothing in this Resolution shall be taken to deprive the House of the power of proceeding against any member according to ancient usages.

10. *Debates on Motions for Adjournment.*—If Mr. Speaker, or the Chairman of a Committee of the whole House, shall be of opinion that a Motion for the Adjournment of a Debate, or of the House, during any debate, or that the Chairman do report progress, or do leave the Chair, is an abuse of the Rules of the House, he may forthwith put the question thereupon from the Chair.

11. *Consideration of a Bill, as amended.*—When the Order of the Day for the Considera-

tion of a Bill, as amended in the Committee of the whole House, has been read, the House do proceed to consider the same without question put, unless the member in charge thereof shall desire to postpone its consideration, or a Motion shall be made to re-commit the Bill.

12. *Notices on going into Committee of Supply.*—That, whenever the Committee of Supply stands as the first Order of the Day on Monday or Thursday, Mr. Speaker shall leave the Chair without putting any question, unless on first going into supply on the Army, Navy, or Civil Service Estimates respectively, or on any Vote of Credit, an Amendment be moved, or question raised, relating to the Estimates proposed to be taken in Supply.

13. That the first seven and the last three of the said Resolutions be Standing Orders of the House.

II. Standing Committees.

1. *Standing Committees on Law and Courts of Justice, Trade, &c.*—That two standing Committees be appointed for the consideration of all Bills relating to Law and Courts of Justice and Legal Procedure, and to Trade, Shipping, and Manufactures, which may, by order of the House, in each case, be committed to them ; and the procedure in such Committees shall be the same as in a Select Committee, unless the House shall otherwise order: Provided, that strangers shall be admitted, except when the Committee shall order them to withdraw: Provided also, That the said Committees shall be excluded from the operation of the Standing Order of July 21st, 1856, and the said Committees shall not sit, whilst the House is sitting, without the order of the House: Provided also, That any Notice of

Amendment to any Clause in a Bill which may be committed to a Standing Committee given by any honourable member in the House shall stand referred to such Committee: Provided also, That twenty be the quorum of such Standing Committees.

2. *Nomination by Committee of Selection.*—That each of the said Standing Committees do consist of not less than sixty, nor more than eighty, members, to be nominated by the Committee of Selection, who shall have regard to the classes of Bills committed to such Committees, to the composition of the House, and to the qualifications of the members selected; and shall have power to discharge members from time to time, and to appoint others in substitution for those so discharged. The Committee of Selection shall also have power to add not more than fifteen members to a Standing Committee in respect of any

Bill referred to it to serve on the Committee during the consideration of such Bill.

3. *Appointment of Chairman.*—The Committee of Selection shall nominate a Chairmen's Panel to consist of not less than four nor more than six members, of whom three shall be a quorum; and the Chairmen's Panel shall appoint from among themselves the Chairman of each Standing Committee, and may change the Chairman so appointed from time to time.

4. *Commitment and Report of Bills.*—That all Bills which shall have been committed to one of the said Standing Committees, shall, when reported to the House, be proceeded with as if they had been reported from a Committee of the whole House: Provided, That the provisions of the Standing Order (Consideration of a Bill as amended), shall

not apply to a Bill reported to the House by a Standing Committee.

5. *Duration of Resolutions.*—That the four preceding Resolutions be Standing Orders of the House until the end of the next Session of Parliament.

The First Rule, disguised under the innocent term of "putting the question," is the famous Closure Rule. Upon this the longest and most acrimonious debate of the session arose. The Conservatives, with a constitutional and long-proved jealousy for freedom of speech, bitterly fought the Government on the question. They foretold a condition of affairs in which debate would become a mockery. The Resolution was called " The Gagging Rule," and it was carried in face of a combination of Conservatives and Parnellites only by a very small majority. In recalling these heated debates, it is almost comical to reflect upon the subsequent history of this portentous rule. It has, in brief, become a dead letter. Speaker and Chairman of Committees alike have shrunk from the responsibility of deciding upon what is "the evident sense of the House," and the consequence has been that, though a score of times occasion has arisen when the Closure Rule might with public advantage have been applied, it has only once been taken from the armoury in which it was placed amid so much foreboding.

The Second Rule, dealing with motions for adjournment before public business, has proved effective in limiting the successes of individual eccentricity. The necessity for it was created by a habit cultivated by Mr. O'Donnell, Mr. Biggar, and one or two other notabilities, of interposing at question time, and moving the adjournment in order to make a speech, the principal design of which was to waste time. This it prohibited, and it also had the effect of investing a motion for adjournment at question time with something more of gravity. It necessitated bustling about before the House met, and securing the co-operation of forty members. There have been several occasions within the last three years when this effort deliberately made has failed. Mr. Parnell, for example, could not always count upon forty supporters for an obstructive motion of this kind. But the regular Opposition were rarely at a loss, and in one week moved the adjournment three times. In the new Parliament, Mr. Parnell, with his increased following, will, of course, be able to set this Rule at nought whenever he pleases.

The Third Rule, limiting opportunities to move or second motions for the adjournment, and contracting openings for discursive debate thereupon, has worked well.

Another most excellent Rule is Number Four, which authorises the Speaker or Chairman to call upon members who challenge his decision to stand up in their places, and if there be less than twenty in a House of forty or upwards, permitting him forthwith to declare the determination of the House or Committee. This Rule, like Number One, was constructed with an eye to Mr. Parnell's party, and during the last Parliament frequently prevented loss of time through vexatious divisions. But with Mr. Parnell's added forces its chances of doing good are practically abrogated.

The Fifth Rule, arming the Speaker or Chairman with power to direct a member guilty of continued irrelevance or tedious repetition to discontinue his speech, has been frequently invoked with wholesome result by Mr. Peel.

Rules Six and Seven each take away an

opportunity of obstructing the progress of a Bill upon technical grounds.

The Half-past Twelve Rule has always been a bone of contention in the House of Commons. It simply provides that after half-past twelve no opposed business may be entered upon. It frequently weighs heavily upon members in charge of a Bill who have been made victims of that blocking system of which Mr. Biggar was Allah and Mr. Warton his Prophet. But these are abuses of a system which beyond doubt conduces to the convenience of the great body of members, and to the proper performance of public business. Before this Rule came into operation members interested in a Bill were bound to hang about till all hours of the night up to the very close of the sitting. Now they may go away at half-past twelve, assured that the object of their particular interest cannot be discussed at the current sitting.

Rule Nine, dealing with the suspension of members, is designed to countercheck an obvious opening for obstruction. If, a member being "named," a resolution were moved for his suspension, it is obvious that, following the ordinary rules, a whole night might be taken up in debating the subject. Rule Nine provides that the question shall be put without amendment, adjournment, or debate. Rule Ten, giving the Speaker or Chairman of Committees power to cut short a discussion on the adjournment, has a promising look about it; but, like the Clôture Rule, it has been allowed to fall into desuetude. Rule Eleven is framed with the object of hastening the progress of Bills; and Rule Twelve seems, upon the face of it, to put an end to the gross waste of time that used to take place on Supply nights. Whenever Supply was put down, members were accustomed to preface it with what is called a notice of amendment, raising all kinds of questions, which must necessarily be discussed before Supply was entered upon. The consequence frequently was that whilst the House of Commons had been engaged in discussing the reason why a postmistress at Ballyhooley was refused an extra pound a year salary, or in debating upon the alleged attack by a police officer on some Irish village, the question of voting millions of money was deferred till after midnight, and taken up by a jaded and angry Committee.

The Rule which, once having gone into Committee of Supply, permits the House on subsequent Mondays and Thursdays straightway to return to Committee, has had much of its usefulness destroyed by an ingenious manœuvre. Members cannot now discuss the postmistress or policeman before going into Committee. But there is nothing against their doing so in Committee; and it has come to pass that the speeches that used to be made with the

Speaker in the Chair are now delivered in Committee, and Supply is no more forward than it used to be.

The scheme of Grand Committees, elaborated in the second portion of the new rules, struck a direct blow of all at obstruction. If, as was intended, all Bills relating to Law and Courts of Justice, to trade, shipping, and manufactures, might be relegated to a Committee sitting up stairs, the strain on the House of Commons would be immensely relieved, and the opportunities of obstruction correspondingly restricted. For one session the Grand Committees had a fair chance, and worked wonders. The Bankruptcy Bill, which had sat like a nightmare over several Parliaments, was disposed of in a single session, and so was the Patents Bill. The obstructionists, alive to the situation, bent all their efforts towards preventing the reappointment of the Grand Committees, and last session the

Government did not even dare to make the proposition. But the principle of devolution illustrated in the action of the Grand Committees is the true principle, and, fully recognised, will eventually work out the salvation of the House of Commons as a business assembly. In some form or other, doubtless in wider bearing than that of Grand Committees, it will have to be adopted by the Legislature.

INDEX.

THE END.

BRADBURY, AGNEW, & CO., PRINTERS, WHITEFRIARS.

SIXPENNY HANDBOOKS OF GAMES.

With Illustrations. (Postage 1*d.*)

Gymnastics.
Chess, with Diagrams, by *G. F. Pardon.*
Whist, by *G. F. Pardon.*
Billiards and Bagatelle, by *G. F. Pardon.*
Draughts and Backgammon, by *G. F. Pardon.*
Cricket.
Cardplayer (The), by *G. F. Pardon.*
Rowing and Sailing.
Riding and Driving.
Archery, Fencing, and Broad-sword.
Riddles.
Manly Exercises: Boxing, Running, Walking, Training, &c., by *Stonehenge, &c.*
Croquet, by *E. Routledge.*
Fishing.
Ball Games.
Conjuring.
Football.
Quoits and Bowls.
Shooting.
Fireworks.
Skating.
Swimming.
Dominoes.

SHILLING HANDBOOKS OF GAMES.

Lawn Tennis, by *Jasper Smythe.*
Base Ball, by *Henry Chadwick.*
Plate Swimming, by *R. H. Wallace-Dunlop, C.B.*

SIXPENNY HOUSEHOLD MANUALS.

Fcap. 8vo, limp. (Postage 1*d.*)

Ladies' Letter-Writer (cloth, 1*s.*)
Gentlemen's Letter-Writer, do.
Village Museum (The); or, How we gathered Profit with Amusement, by *Rev. G. T. Hoare.*
How to Cook Apples in 100 Different Ways, by *G. Hill.*
How to Cook and Serve Eggs in 100 Different Ways, by *Georgiana Hill.*
How to Cook Rabbits in 124 Different Ways, by *Georgiana Hill.*
Every-Day Blunders in Speaking.
Lovers' Letter-Writer (cloth, 1*s.*)
Cholera, by *Dr. Lankester.*
Home Nursing.
How to Make Soup in 100 Ways
How to Cook Onions in 100 Ways.
Recipe Book.
How to Dress Salads.
How to Make Cakes.
How to Dress Vegetables.
Lady Housekeeper's Poultry Yard.
How to Make Pickles in 100 Ways.
Francatelli's Cookery.
Invalid's Cook.
How to Hash Cold Meat in 100 Ways.
Puddings, How to Make in 100 Ways.

BOOKS FOR THE COUNTRY.

Fcap. 8vo, with numerous Illustrations, in fancy boards, or printed cloth boards, **One Shilling** each. (Postage *2d.*)

Angling and Where to Go, by *Blakey.*

Pigeons and Rabbits, by *E. S. Delamer*, with Illustrations by H. Weir.

Shooting, by *Blakey*, Illustrations by H. Weir.

The Sheep: Domestic Breeds and Treatment, by *W. C. L. Martin*, Illust. by Harvey.

Flax and Hemp: Their Culture and Manipulation, by *Delamer*, plates.

Poultry Yard, by *E. Watts*, illustrated by H. Weir.

The Horse, by *Cecil*, illustrated by Wells.

Bees: Their Habits and Management, by *Rev. J. G. Wood.*

Cage and Singing Birds, by *H. G. Adams.*

Small Farms, and How they ought to be Managed, by *M. Doyle.*

Kitchen Garden, by *E. S. Delamer.*

Flower Garden, by ditto.

Farmer's Manual of Live Stock.

Field and Garden Plants.

Common Objects of the Sea-Shore.

Common Objects of the Country.

Woodlands, Heaths, and Hedges, by *W. S. Coleman.*

British Ferns, by *Thomas Moore, F.L.S.*, bds., with Coloured Plates.

Favourite Flowers.

British Birds' Eggs and Nests, by the *Rev. J. C. Atkinson.*

The Pig: How to Choose, Breed, Rear, Keep, and Cure, by *Samuel Sidney.*

British Butterflies, by *Coleman.*

Hints for Farmers.

Fresh and Salt Water Aquarium, by the *Rev. J. G. Wood, M.A.*

British Moths, by *Rev. J. G. Wood.*

Window Gardening, by *A. Meikle.*

Homing or Carrier Pigeon: Its History, Management, and Method of Training, by *W. B. Tegetmeier.*

Geology for the Million.

Cottage Garden, by *A. Meikle.*

Fly Fishing, by *H. C. Pennell.*

Bottom Fishing, by *H. C. Pennell.*

Trolling, by *H. C. Pennell.*

Domestic Cat, by *Dr. Gordon Stables.*

Rinks and Rollers, a Guide to the Skating Rink.

The Canary, by *J. G. Barnesby.*

Plate-Swimming, by *R. H. Dunlop, C.B.*

The Colorado Beetle.

Lawn Tennis, by *Jasper Smythe.*

Roses and How to Grow Them, with Illustrations.

1s. 6d. each.

Cattle: Their History and various Breeds, Management, Treatment, and Diseases, by *W. C. L. Martin*, revised by *W. & H. Raynbird.*

Dogs: Their Management in Health and Disease, by *Edward Mayhew, M.R.C.V.S.*, with Illustrations.

2s. each.

The Rat, with Anecdotes, by *Uncle James.*

Wild Flowers: Where to Find and How to Know them, by *Spencer Thomson*, illustrated.

Rarey on Horse Taming.

BOOKS FOR THE COUNTRY, *continued.*

Haunts of the Wild Flowers, by *Anne Pratt.*
Agricultural Chemistry, by *Alfred Sibson, F.C.S.*
Our Native Song Birds, by *Barnesby.*
Walton and Cotton's Angler, with additions by *Ephemera.*
Our Farm of Four Acres.
The Stud Farm, by *Cecil.*
Mr. Mechi's How to Farm Profitably. 2nd series, fcap. 8vo.
——— 3rd series.
Calendar of the Months, by *Rev. J. G. Wood, M.A.*

BOOKS FOR THE COUNTRY, FINE EDITION.

Printed on superior paper, with the Plates printed in Colours, except where marked *, fcap. 8vo, bevelled boards, gilt edges, 3s. 6d. each.

Wood's Common Objects of the Sea-Shore.
Wood's Common Objects of the Country.
Our Woodlands, Heaths, and Hedges.
Moore's British Ferns and Allied Plants.
Coleman's British Butterflies, 200 figures.
Atkinson's British Birds' Eggs and Nests.
Thomson's (Spencer) Wild Flowers.
Wood's (Rev. J. G.) Common Objects of the Microscope.
Anne Pratt's Haunts of Wild Flowers.
Delamer's Kitchen and Flower Garden.
Wood's (Rev. J. G.) Fresh and Salt-Water Aquarium.
Wood's (Rev. J. G.) Common British Moths.
Wood's (Rev. J. G.) Common British Beetles.
*Bechstein's Chamber and Cage Birds.
*Calendar of the Months, by the *Rev. J. G. Wood.*
*Walton and Cotton's Angler.
Roses: A Handbook of How, When, and Where to Purchase, Propagate, and Plant Them, with 8 pages Coloured Illustrations.
Gardening at a Glance, by *George Glenny*, with many Illustrations and Coloured Plates.

* These have plain woodcuts.

RECITERS AND READINGS.

In fancy covers, price 1s. each. (Postage *2d.*)

Carpenter's Comic Reciter.
——— Popular Reciter.
Routledge's Comic Readings.
——— Popular Readings.
Routledge's Dramatic Readings.
———Temperance Reciter.
Ready-made Speeches.

RUBY SERIES. *1s., 1s. 6d.*, and *2s.*

A Collection of Stories mostly of a Religious character, comprising Works of Miss WETHERELL, Rev. J. H. INGRAHAM, Miss CUMMINS, Mrs. STOWE, and others. *See Catalogue of Religious Books.*

ROUTLEDGE'S USEFUL LIBRARY, in Shilling Volumes,

including Cookery and Housekeeping.

Ladies' and Gentlemen's Letter Writer, Forms of Address, &c., cloth boards.
Home Book of Domestic Economy, by *Anne Bowman.*
Common Things of Every-Day Life, by ditto.
Rundell's Domestic Cookery, unabridged.
Tricks of Trade in the Adulteration of Food and Physic.
Common Objects of the Microscope, by the *Rev. J. G. Wood*, with 400 Illustrations by Tuffen West, boards.
Hints for the Table, by *J. Timbs.*
How to Make Money, by *Freedley.*
Infant Nursing, by *Mrs. Pedley.*
Practical Housekeeping, by *Mrs. Pedley.*
A Manual of Weathercasts and Storm Prognostics.
The Commercial Letter-Writer.
Ready-Made Speeches.
The Dinner Question, by *Tabitha Tickletooth.*
The Book of Proverbs, cloth.
2,000 Familiar Quotations, cloth.
The Book of Phrases and Mottoes, cloth.
500 Abbreviations made Intelligible, cloth.
How to Economise like a Lady, by the Author of "How to Dress on £15 a Year."
Buckmaster's Cookery; Lectures delivered at South Kensington, cloth, 2*s.* 6*d.*
How to Dress on £15 a Year as a Lady, by a Lady.
Guide to London, revised to 1878.
Tables and Chairs, a Guide to Economical Furnishing, by the Author of "How to Dress on £15 a Year."
The Competitor's Manual for Spelling Bees.
Breakfast, Luncheon, and Tea, by *Marion Harland.*
Soyer's Shilling Cookery for the People.
How we Managed without Servants, by a Lady who can Help.
Shilling Manual of Etiquette.
Knots and How to Tie Them, by *J. T. Burgess*, Illustrated.
The Pleasures of House Building, a Story of Struggle and Adventure, by *J. Ford Mackenzie.*
The Electric Light, by *T. C. Hepworth*, with 35 Illustrations.

1s. 6d. each.

Landmarks of the History of England, by *Rev. James White*, boards.
Landmarks of the History of Greece, by *Rev. James White*, boards.
Gazetteer (The) of Great Britain and Ireland.
Mrs. Rundell's Cookery, fcap., cloth.

SPORTING BOOKS.

Cheap Editions, in fancy boards, 2s. each; or in cloth, 2s. 6d.

John Mytton's Life.
Jorrocks' Jaunts.
Scrutator on Foxhunting.
Scrutator's Horses and Hounds.
The Tommiebeg Shootings.
Sporting Sketches.
Nimrod's Northern Tour.

www.ingramcontent.com/pod-product-compliance
Lightning Source LLC
Chambersburg PA
CBHW030616270326
41927CB00007B/1203
* 9 7 8 3 7 4 4 6 7 9 4 6 6 *